"This book renewed my faith in God's daily hand in my life. Each page felt like a personal conversation with the Spirit."
— Mary J., Sydney, Australia

"Reading this devotional in the quiet of my mornings has brought me peace I didn't know I was missing. A treasure for anyone seeking Christ."
— Lukas A., Stockholm, Sweden

"As someone who often doubted whether I had spiritual gifts, this book showed me they were already in my life. It gave me hope."
— Carlos M., Provo, USA

"Deeply moving. The journaling prompts opened up a new level of prayer and reflection for me. I feel closer to Christ than ever."
— Tunde O., Helena, USA

"Beautifully written, practical, and Spirit-filled. I bought extra copies to share with friends in my ward."
— Jacob W., Salt Lake City, USA

"This devotional connected scripture to my daily struggles in such a gentle, powerful way. Truly a gift."
— Angela C., Los Angeles, USA

"Every page reminded me that God is aware of me personally. This devotional has become part of my daily study."
— Sarah L., Dallas, USA

"The way spiritual gifts are explained here gave me new eyes to see how God has always been guiding me. I couldn't put it down."
— Rina P., Boise, USA

"I've read many devotionals, but this one feels different—it invites me to notice the small, everyday ways God is working in my life. A true blessing."
— Daniel R., Chicago, USA

EVERY GOOD GIFT COMES FROM OUR HEAVENLY FATHER.

My Gift to You; Discovering How the Lord Works Through You
Copyright © 2025 / First edition by Emmaline Hoffmeister

All rights reserved.

No portion of this book may be reproduced, distributed, or transmitted in any form or by any means, including photocopying, recording, or other electronic or mechanical methods, without the prior written permission of the publisher, except in the case of brief quotations embodied in critical reviews and certain other noncommercial uses permitted by U.S. copyright law.

The mention of scripture included in this work are the property of their respective copyright holders. The scriptures are used here for creative purposes under fair use, and no infringement is intended. All scripture references in this work are taken from the King James Version of the Holy Bible and the standard works of The Church of Jesus Christ of Latter-day Saints, including the Book of Mormon, the Doctrine and Covenants, the Pearl of Great Price, and other standard church works.

ISBNs
eBook: 978-1-936850-53-2
Paperback: 978-1-936850-51-8

Jacket, cover, and interior design by Emmaline Hoffmeister
Editing by PWA Editing Services
Cover image © Nittaya: Jesus Christ and white dove as a symbol of the Holy Spirit, Watercolor style. (Adobe Stock)
Fonts AT Avalaqus Serif, EB Garamond, Passions Conflict
Author photo © MJ Hodges Photography

For permissions requests, write to the publisher at:
Rhemalda Publishing
Attn: Publicist / Emmaline Hoffmeister
101 Rainbow Dr. #9867, Livingston, TX 77399

Also By

EMMALINE HOFFMEISTER

STANDALONE DEVOTIONAL BOOKS
Let Him In; Daily Devotionals to Hear Him, Follow Him, and Become Like Him
(Devotionals for Latter-day Saints)

I Am His; 100 Affirmations of Who I Am in Christ
(Non-Denominational Christian—King James Version of the Bible)

My Gift to You; Discovering How the Lord Works Through You
(Devotionals for Latter-day Saints)

STANDALONE BOOKS
(LDS Christian Fiction)
Left Behind

JANE AUSTEN VARIATIONS
(Historical Romance)
Longbourn's Unexpected Matchmaker ✶ *Pemberley Mistletoe* ✶
Threat of Scandal ✶ *The Illegitimate Heir* ✶ *Scent of Desire*

SHALESLIP MANOR COLLECTION
(Historical Romantic Suspense)
Narrow Escape ✶ *True Lies* ✶ *Burden of Innocence*

Contents

Introduction	IX
How to Use This Book	X
Tips for Getting the Most Out of This Book	XI
Epigraph	XIII
Testimony	XIV
Opening	3
Week 1	9
Week 2	33
Week 3	57
Week 4	81
Closing	105
Keep Studying Spiritual Gifts	110

Introduction

SPIRITUAL GIFTS HAVE ALWAYS been close to my heart.

They have guided me when I felt lost. Comforted me when I felt unseen. Strengthened me when I felt weak. The more I've come to recognize them—not just the bold ones, but the quiet ones too—the more deeply personal and sacred this topic has become.

This book was born from that love. From the realization that spiritual gifts aren't rare privileges or distant ideals. They're part of our covenant walk with Jesus Christ. They are the fingerprints of heaven on our everyday lives.

I've learned that spiritual gifts often don't come all at once. They unfold as we seek them. They whisper through our efforts to serve. They bloom in places we least expect. Writing these devotionals has deepened my gratitude for the Spirit's companionship and taught me that when we *look* for God's hand, we *find* it—often in the unique gifts He's placed inside each of us.

My prayer is that this book will help you do the same.

As you read, reflect, and write, I hope you'll discover more clearly how the Lord is already at work within you, and how He's inviting you to grow even more. Your spiritual gifts are real. They are needed. And they are yours for the asking.

How to Use This Book

THIS DEVOTIONAL IS DESIGNED to guide you into a deeper connection with Jesus Christ by helping you recognize His hand in your life through scripture, reflection, and spiritual gifts. Each entry follows a simple and meaningful pattern to help you pause, invite the Spirit, and apply what you learn.

Here's what you'll find in every devotional:
- **Scripture** – A verse or passage from the standard works of The Church of Jesus Christ of Latter-day Saints, grounding your study in the word of God.

- **Doctrinal Reflection** – A short thought to help you understand and apply the principle, blending scripture, testimony, and everyday examples.

- **Invitation** – A simple action to take that day, designed to help you live what you've learned and open your heart to the Spirit.

- **Journaling Prompt** – A question or reflection starter to help you capture your impressions and recognize the Lord's hand in your life.

- **Affirmation** – A statement of truth to speak or write as a reminder of God's love and power in your life.

Tips for Getting the Most Out of This Book

- **Go at your own pace.** You can study one devotional a day, revisit favorites, or use the book as needed.

- **Pray before and after.** Ask the Lord to open your heart as you read and to help you recognize the spiritual gifts He is already giving you.

- **Write your impressions.** Use the journaling prompts as a place to record your testimony, experiences, and growth.

- **Return often.** Each time you revisit a devotional, you may notice something new as the Spirit teaches you in different seasons of your life.

THIS BOOK IS NOT meant to be rushed. It is meant to be lived. Let each page be a quiet moment with the Lord—a chance to hear Him, to see His gifts in your life, and to feel His love more deeply.

Each gift is a signature of heaven, etched across our lives. Every blessing is His handwriting, reminding us that we are known and loved. Spiritual gifts are not rare treasures for a chosen few, but daily evidence that God is near—whispered assurances, sacred strengths, and quiet miracles. Heaven speaks, and through every gift the Spirit signs His name upon our hearts.

Testimony

I KNOW GOD LIVES and that He loves His children. Through His Son, Jesus Christ, He has given us gifts of the Spirit—*divine blessings that are both personal and powerful*. These gifts are not limited to prophets or apostles of old; they are present and available to each and every person who is alive today. They are given to ordinary disciples of Jesus Christ like you and me, not for our glory, but to bless, to heal, to strengthen, and to build up the body of Christ.

I have felt the reality of these gifts in my life. In moments of loneliness, the Lord has sent words of comfort through others. In seasons of weakness, I have found strength that was not my own. At times when I have prayed for guidance, quiet impressions have come that carried me in the exact direction I needed to go. Each of these moments has been a witness to me that God knows me personally and is mindful of my needs.

I have also learned that one of the greatest gifts is personal revelation. Heavenly Father speaks to His children, not only through prophets, but through the still, small voice of the Holy Ghost. Sometimes His answers come as a clear impression, other times as a quiet peace that confirms the path is right. I know He hears every prayer, and that His guidance is real.

I have seen miracles—large and small—that confirm the Lord's hand in daily life. Some have been unmistakable answers to desperate prayers. Others have been subtle mercies that might be overlooked unless the Spirit opened my eyes to recognize them. The more I have sought the Lord, the more I have seen that nothing in life is truly "ordinary." God is constantly at work, weaving tender mercies into my days.

I believe spiritual gifts come in many forms: the gift of faith, the gift of discernment, the gift to comfort, the gift to teach, the gift of healing, and countless others. Each gift is a signature of heaven, given to remind us that we are never alone.

I bear witness that Jesus Christ is the giver of all good gifts. Through Him, every one of us can receive what we need most. As we discover, develop, and use our spiritual gifts, we will come to know Him more deeply, see His hand more clearly, and feel His love more fully.

In the name of Jesus Christ, amen.

Opening

EVERY GOOD GIFT COMES from our Heavenly Father. He is a God who loves to give, and His blessings are scattered across our days in both ordinary and extraordinary ways. Some gifts are easy to see—answered prayers, tender mercies, moments of peace. Others are quieter, tucked into the rhythm of daily life, waiting for us to notice.

This book is an invitation to pause long enough to see those gifts. Each day offers a scripture, a reflection, and a place to turn your heart toward Christ. Some days may feel familiar, like truths you've always known deep down. Others may spark something new, nudging you to see yourself and your discipleship differently.

The Spirit whispers in simple ways: in the warmth of a child's hug, in strength you didn't know you had, in the courage to forgive, in the quiet assurance that you are not alone. These are gifts—evidence that God is with you.

As you begin this journey, I invite you to come with openness and expectation. Pray before you read. Write what the Spirit brings to your mind. Let these pages become a conversation between you and the Lord.

My prayer is that in the next thirty days, you will not only *learn* about the gifts of the Spirit but *experience* them, see them in yourself, recognize them in others, and let them draw you closer to the Giver of every good gift.

Day 1

> *"And all these gifts come from God, for the benefit of the children of God."*
> Doctrine and Covenants 46:26

WE OFTEN THINK OF spiritual gifts as things reserved for prophets, pioneers, or especially righteous people. But the truth is, they're for *you*. Today. Right now. Spiritual gifts are one of the clearest signs that God knows you personally and is actively guiding your life.

The scriptures tell us spiritual gifts are given *for our benefit*. Not to show off. Not to compete. Not even necessarily to stand out. But to bless. To heal. To guide. They are the Lord's way of whispering, "I'm with you. I've equipped you. You are not alone in this."

A friend once told me about a particularly discouraging day when she felt invisible, like her efforts didn't matter to anyone. Out of nowhere, another friend texted her a message that pierced straight to her heart: "I felt prompted to tell you that what you're doing matters. Don't stop." That moment changed her day. She said it felt like the Lord Himself had reached out. God had spoken to her friend's heart, telling her exactly what she needed in that moment.

And her friend chose to listen. She stepped forward, using her gift of encouragement to bless in a way no one else could have.

That's the power of spiritual gifts: **when we yield to the whisperings of the Lord, we become His hands, His voice, and His heart for someone else.**

You may not know what all of your spiritual gifts are. That's okay. This journey will help you recognize them in yourself and in others. And when you do, you'll start to see them for what they really are: *a signature of heaven, written across your life.*

Sometimes these gifts bless others through us, and sometimes they bless us directly. The Lord gives us these gifts because He loves us, and because He knows exactly what will help us endure, grow, and press forward.

Paul wrote, "But the manifestation of the Spirit is given to every man to profit withal." (1 Corinthians 12:7). That means you, too, have been given divine gifts meant to uplift, strengthen, and bring light to the people around you.

I invite you to pray and ask: "Lord, help me see the gifts You've placed in my life. Help me recognize when they are at work and give me courage to use them." He will answer. And when He does, you'll discover that spiritual gifts are not distant or rare—they are alive in you, today.

Invitation:

Pause and pray today. Ask Heavenly Father to help you recognize one spiritual gift He's given you or used *through* someone else to bless you.

Journaling Prompt:

When have you felt the Spirit work *through* your gift to bless your life or the life of another?

Affirmation:

God has gifted me with spiritual gifts. Through His Spirit, I can easily recognize them, and I see His hand already at work in my life.

Week 1

God Gives Good Gifts

SPIRITUAL GIFTS ARE AMONG the clearest expressions of God's love. They are not rewards for righteousness, nor trophies of worth, they are manifestations of grace. Each gift is handpicked by a wise and loving Heavenly Father, tailored to fit our divine identity, our earthly needs, and our eternal potential.

As we begin this journey, we center our hearts on the Giver: the One who delights in blessing His children and empowering them through the Spirit. Every gift we receive—from discernment to healing, from patience to testimony—bears the signature of God.

This week is about remembering that your spiritual gifts are not random or rare. They are deeply personal evidence that you are known, loved, and invited into partnership with the divine.

Day 2

> "Every good gift and every perfect gift is from above, and cometh down from the Father of lights, with whom is no variableness, neither shadow of turning."
>
> James 1:17

HAVE YOU EVER RECEIVED a gift so personal that it made you feel deeply seen? That's what spiritual gifts are meant to be. They're not one-size-fits-all—they're heaven-tailored. James reminds us that every good and perfect gift comes from above. That means every spiritual gift you or I have ever received has been chosen by a loving Heavenly Father who knows exactly what will bless us and those around us.

Sometimes we miss these gifts because they don't look the way we expect. We're waiting for miracles or visions, and instead we receive insight during a sacrament talk or feel peace during a chaotic day. The Spirit whispers, and we're looking for thunder.

But God's gifts are always good. Always perfect for the moment. And always given with love. Sometimes they steady us in private, sometimes they reach us through another person, but they always arrive with divine intent.

One Sunday I watched a young woman bear her testimony. She didn't speak loudly or eloquently, but there was something in her quiet voice that pierced my heart. I realized I was witnessing the gift of testimony in action—not dramatic, but deeply moving. It was exactly what my spirit needed.

That moment reminded me that spiritual gifts are not measured by volume or attention, but by impact. A single phrase, a single word of the Spirit, can reach deeper than the most polished speech.

And here's the beautiful truth: because God is unchanging—the "Father of lights, with whom is no variableness"—His gifts are constant too. He knows when to send them, how to shape them, and why you need them. They are His way of reminding you that He sees you, He knows you, and He loves you.

Spiritual gifts are given to remind us that God is real. They don't just prove His existence—they express His nature. He is generous. He is good. And He gives because He loves.

Invitation:

Look back on the last few days. Can you identify one moment where you saw a spiritual gift in action, either in yourself or someone else?

Journaling Prompt:

What is one gift from God that you've received recently—spiritual or otherwise—that reminded you of His love?

Affirmation:

God gives me good and perfect gifts because He knows me and loves me personally.

Day 3

> *"For all have not every gift given unto them; for there are many gifts, and to every man is given a gift by the Spirit of God."*
> Doctrine and Covenants 46:11

THERE'S A LIE THAT slips in quietly: the thought that spiritual gifts are for other people. The prophets. The Relief Society president. That ultra-spiritual friend who wakes up at 5 a.m. to study her scriptures. But not you. Not someone with flaws, doubts, or an ordinary life.

Doctrine and Covenants 46:11 pushes back against that lie. It doesn't say *some* are given gifts. It says *every man*—meaning every woman, every teenager, every new convert, every overworked parent, every single person who has ever walked, or ever will walk, upon God's beautiful earth—is given a gift by the Spirit of God.

Let that sink in: you've already been gifted.

It might be the gift of believing Christ's words. Or the ability to comfort others. Maybe it's a spiritual sensitivity to music, or a natural ability to bring people together. Perhaps it's the gift of discernment, the quiet strength to endure trials with faith, the ability to teach with clarity, or the courage to bear simple testimony at just the right moment. Some may feel prompted to pray with power, while others naturally lift burdens with service. These gifts don't always come with fanfare, but every one is divine.

A friend once told me about the first time she began noticing her own spiritual gifts. At first, they didn't feel impressive. She had a knack for remembering every detail a person shared with her, and then acting on promptings related to those details to help them feel seen and loved. For years, she didn't think of that as a gift, it just felt natural. But over time she began to notice something: those "small" actions often arrived at the exact moment someone needed encouragement or hope. That wasn't coincidence. That was the Spirit. As she watched how those little remembrances lifted others, she started to see God's fingerprints all over them.

That's the beautiful reality: ***you don't have to be flawless to be gifted.*** Spiritual gifts aren't earned—they are given. And God delights in giving them to ordinary people, because He delights in doing extraordinary things through them.

You don't need to wait to be gifted. You already are. The invitation is to *recognize* the gift, *receive* it with gratitude, and *use* it with faith.

Invitation:

Pray specifically to understand one spiritual gift the Lord has already given you, and to see how it's shown up in your life before now.

Journaling Prompt:

What is one ability or pattern in your life that could be a spiritual gift you hadn't noticed before?

Affirmation:

I have already been given a spiritual gift by the Spirit of God, and I am learning to see it.

Day 4

> *"To some it is given by the Holy Ghost to know that Jesus Christ is the Son of God, and that he was crucified for the sins of the world."*
> Doctrine and Covenants 46:13

WE SOMETIMES THINK SPIRITUAL gifts should be dramatic—visions, healings, prophecy. But some of the most powerful gifts are the simplest. Just knowing that Jesus is the Christ is a gift. Just believing Him is a gift.

In a world that questions and doubts, having a quiet confidence in the Savior is a miracle in itself. The world may call it naïve or outdated, but heaven calls it sacred.

A man once told me about a time when he felt spiritually dry, as if the heavens were silent and his prayers were not doing much. One day, while walking outside, he felt a quiet assurance press into his heart: *You still believe in Me.* That realization choked him up. It was not dramatic or overwhelming. It was not accompanied by thunder or angels. It was a whisper that settled so gently he almost could have missed it, but it was real, and it was enough. It was not a vision or a powerful manifestation, just a quiet assurance that he still believed. He still hoped. That, he realized, was the gift.

Faith is never small to God. The Holy Ghost plants and nourishes it, sometimes in dramatic ways, but often in whispers that steady us when nothing else can. Even the smallest seed of testimony has divine power. As Alma taught, "... ***even if ye can no more than desire to believe, let this desire work in you,*** ..."(Alma 32:27). That desire itself is a gift.

Sometimes we discount that gift because it feels too small, but to God it is precious. Faith, however fragile, is still faith—and He promises that if we hold onto it, He will cause it to grow.

So hold on to it. Feed it. Share it. And trust that even the smallest seed of testimony can grow into something eternal.

Invitation:

Acknowledge your faith today—no matter how small it feels. Offer a prayer of thanks for the spiritual gift of belief in Christ.

Journaling Prompt:

When have you felt the gift of belief in Christ sustain you, especially during times of uncertainty or quiet?

Affirmation:

My faith in Jesus Christ is a spiritual gift, and it is growing stronger every day.

Day 5

> *"Now there are diversities of gifts, but the same Spirit."*
>
> 1 Corinthians 12:4

IT'S EASY TO LOOK at someone else's strengths and think, *Why didn't I get that gift?* Maybe they teach with power, or they speak with wisdom, or they seem to know exactly what to say in a priesthood blessing. We might wonder if we somehow missed out.

But here's what the scriptures say: there are many gifts—and while they differ, they all come from the same Spirit. That means there's intention behind the diversity. Each one of us is given a spiritual gift, uniquely suited to our path and our purpose. **What looks like "ordinary ability" to you may actually be extraordinary in God's eyes, because He placed it in you for a reason.**

Comparison is a clever thief. It can steal our gratitude and blind us to what we do have. But if we shift our view, we can see that spiritual gifts weren't meant to compete, they're meant to complement. The Lord distributes them among us so we can serve and strengthen one another.

Years ago, when I served in a Relief Society presidency, the president shared an experience that stayed with me. She told us about a ward council where every leader had a totally different way of approaching a challenge. Some were warm and nurturing, others were bold and visionary. She noticed how each person's spiritual gift added something the group needed. Together, they were stronger. She said in that moment she realized the Spirit is a master builder, weaving our gifts together like bricks in a temple wall—each one small on its own, but essential to the strength of the whole.

That's how the Lord designed it. Paul taught that just as the body has many members, each part is needed for the whole to function (1 Corinthians 12:12–20). Your gift may not be flashy, but it matters. Without it, something vital would be missing.

And here's the good news: you don't have to be someone else to be valuable. God didn't intend for you to copy another person's gifts. He intended for you to lean into your own, trusting that they are enough, and that when combined with the gifts of others, they build something far greater than you could alone.

You were meant to fill a space only you can fill. And God knew that when He gave that specific gift to you. The very fact that it was placed in your life is evidence of His trust—that you, and no one else, were called to carry it.

Invitation:

Look for one spiritual gift in someone else today and thank Heavenly Father for the way it blesses your life or your ward.

Journaling Prompt:

Identify one of your spiritual gifts. Then reflect on this question: How can that gift complement or strengthen someone else?

Affirmation:

My gift has a purpose. God gave it to me to bless others and help build His kingdom.

Day 6

> *"And by the power of the Holy Ghost ye may know the truth of all things."*
>
> Moroni 10:5

MORONI'S FINAL CHAPTER READS like a spiritual treasure map. He invites us to come unto Christ, to ask God for answers, and to believe in spiritual gifts. Then he assures us that through the Holy Ghost, we can know the truth of all things.

Think about that promise. The Spirit can testify, reveal, comfort, warn, and confirm. No matter your question—about doctrine, direction, or daily decisions—the Holy Ghost can help you find truth. That is a spiritual gift in itself.

Sometimes we wait for answers to come in dramatic ways, but Moroni reminds us that the still, small voice is enough. The ability to recognize that whisper is a gift worth seeking and treasuring.

A friend once told me about a decision that kept him up at night. He made pros and cons lists. He fasted. He wore out his knees in prayer. Then one morning, as he was reading the Book of Mormon, a verse he had read a hundred times before suddenly came alive. In that moment, he knew exactly what he needed to do. That clarity—that witness—was the Holy Ghost doing what He does best.

The Spirit doesn't just give truth once and move on; He reminds, reaffirms, and restores it when doubts creep in. Jesus promised His disciples that the Comforter would bring all things to your remembrance. That means we can lean on Him not only to discover truth but also to hold on to it.

> *"But the Comforter, which is the Holy Ghost, whom the Father will send in my name, he shall teach you all things, **and bring all things to your remembrance**, whatsoever I have said unto you."*
>
> John 14:26

God is not hiding. The gifts of the Spirit are real and available, and Moroni pleads with us to seek them with real intent. The whisper is enough. The Spirit is enough. And through Him, you can always find truth.

Invitation:

Ask in prayer today for the Holy Ghost to confirm something you already believe—to let you feel again that it's true.

Journaling Prompt:

What truth has the Holy Ghost helped you know in your heart, even when logic alone wasn't enough?

Affirmation:

The Holy Ghost helps me recognize truth, and that gift is always available when I seek it.

Day 7

> *"Be thou humble; and the Lord thy God shall lead thee by the hand, and give thee answer to thy prayers."*
>
> Doctrine and Covenants 112:10

SPIRITUAL GIFTS THRIVE IN humble soil. The more we seek to recognize God's hand in our lives, the more open we become to receiving His gifts. Humility isn't self-doubt. It's spiritual readiness. It's the willingness to say, "I may not have all the answers, but I know where to turn."

The proud believe they must do everything alone. The humble know that every good thing—including spiritual gifts—flows from God. That attitude opens the heavens. Humility is what makes room for grace. It clears away the noise of self-importance and creates space for the whisperings of the Spirit. Without it, we can become so focused on our own strength that we miss the gentle nudges of God's hand.

I remember watching a young father stand to bear his testimony. He started by saying, "I'm not good at this. I don't know what to say." But then he shared a simple story about reading the scriptures with his toddler. The Spirit filled the room. His humility let the gift of testimony shine without pretense or polish. Everyone felt it. It wasn't his eloquence that mattered; it was his sincerity. **The Lord took his offering, small as it seemed to him, and magnified it so it could touch every heart present.**

Sometimes the best way to grow our spiritual gifts is simply to be teachable. To admit we don't know everything. To ask. To listen. And to trust that if we're open, God will always fill our hands. As the Savior taught, *"Yea, blessed are the poor in spirit who come unto me, for theirs is the kingdom of heaven."* (3 Nephi 12:3) A humble heart is an invitation for heaven to act. It is like rich soil, ready for seeds to be planted, watered, and nurtured until they bring forth fruit.

The truth is, God isn't looking for perfect polish—He's looking for willing vessels. When we approach Him in humility, He magnifies our small offerings, making them enough to bless and strengthen others. That's the miracle of humility: it transforms weakness into strength, ordinary into sacred, and simple faith into spiritual power.

Invitation:

Spend a few quiet moments in prayer today, asking the Lord to teach you something new about your spiritual gifts, and to help you receive it with a humble heart.

Journaling Prompt:

How has humility helped you become more receptive to the Spirit and more aware of God's gifts?

Affirmation:

As I stay humble, the Lord leads me, teaches me, and fills my life with spiritual gifts.

Day 8

> *"For all have not every gift given unto them; for there are many gifts, and to every man is given a gift by the Spirit of God.*
>
> *To some is given one, and to some is given another, that all may be profited thereby."*
> Doctrine and Covenants 46:11–12

AS WE FINISH THIS first week, let this truth settle into your soul: **you are already gifted.** The Lord isn't waiting for you to qualify yourself or reach some spiritual milestone. He's already placed divine gifts in your life—because He trusts you and because He loves those you'll bless through them.

That's the pattern: *He gives, we receive, and then we share.* His kingdom moves forward as ordinary disciples, one by one, choose to act on the gifts they've been given. Your offering may seem small, but in God's hands it becomes part of something eternal.

If you've spent the last few days wondering what your spiritual gifts are, don't be discouraged. Sometimes recognition comes slowly, but the Lord is patient. What matters most is the desire to *notice* and the willingness to *act* on what you learn. With time, clarity will come. Often, we only recognize a gift in hindsight—when we see how it lifted someone else or carried us through a hard moment. Keep watching. Keep listening. **The Spirit delights in revealing what is already there.**

I once heard someone say, "Spiritual gifts are like stars, you don't always see them until it gets dark." That thought has stayed with me. Sometimes our gifts shine brightest in the hard seasons, the quiet acts, or the unseen sacrifices. They show up just when someone needs a little light. And often, the very gift you overlook in yourself is the one someone else has been praying for.

So, trust the Giver. He knows what He's doing. And He's already working through you, even if you don't see it yet. Lean into that trust, and let this week's devotionals be the foundation for the journey ahead. The Lord doesn't just give gifts, He gives Himself. And when you walk with Him, you'll never walk without light.

Invitation:

Review your notes and reflections from this week. What patterns do you see? What has the Spirit gently emphasized to your heart?

Journaling Prompt:

Which spiritual gift from this week feels closest to your heart right now, and why?

Affirmation:

God has gifted me with purpose. I am learning to see, receive, and share those gifts with love.

Week 2

Recognizing the Gifts in Everyday Life

SPIRITUAL GIFTS DON'T ALWAYS come with fanfare or dramatic manifestations. More often, they arrive quietly—woven into our daily interactions, prayers, and thoughts. This week is an invitation to notice them. To see how the Spirit operates not just in the sacred, but in the simple.

A moment of clarity, a comforting word, a patient heart, a whisper of personal revelation, a healing gesture—these are all spiritual gifts in motion. The Lord didn't intend for His gifts to remain hidden or only appear on the stage for big moments. He placed them within us to bless homes, conversations, callings, and communities. They are designed to be practical, timely, and personal, just as much for your workplace as for the temple.

As we slow down and pay attention, we begin to recognize how deeply present these divine gifts are in our ordinary, holy lives. The Spirit is already working in ways we may have overlooked, and as we train our eyes to see, we'll start to discover that heaven is far closer than we realized.

Day 9

"For to one is given by the Spirit the word of wisdom; to another the word of knowledge by the same Spirit;"

1 Corinthians 12:8

SOME GIFTS ARE VISIBLE. Others unfold quietly in the mind and heart, like the gift of knowledge. It's not just about having a good memory or getting the right answers. It's about spiritual insight. A deep knowing that comes from the Spirit, not from studying alone.

This gift often feels ordinary. You're reading the scriptures and a verse suddenly feels alive. Or you hear a talk and understand something you've never noticed before. Or you're counseling with a friend and truth pours out of you, and you know it didn't come from you. It is a light that turns simple words into revelation, familiar doctrines into living truth, and ordinary conversations into moments of divine direction.

Years ago, a friend told me about a calling that felt way beyond him. He didn't have the right experience—life, church, college, work—none of it had prepared him. He didn't feel qualified. But again and again, as he studied and prepared, understanding would come. Ideas he hadn't thought of. Scriptures he hadn't planned to share. He learned to recognize those moments as spiritual knowledge. It was the Holy Ghost helping him know what he needed to know, when he needed to know it. The more he leaned on the Spirit, the more he realized it wasn't just about him being prepared, it was about the Lord preparing hearts, including his own.

As I write these devotional books, I see the same thing happening in me. The process feels familiar, the same kind of study, pondering, and quiet impressions that once carried him through that calling are now guiding me as well. These pages are expanding my knowledge in the very same way: *through steady learning, spiritual insight, and the gentle tutoring of the Spirit.*

You may not see this gift as dramatic, but it is, and it is deeply personal to the one who has this gift. It shows up in classrooms and kitchens. In gospel conversations and quiet moments of study. It gives you confidence to speak when you feel unsure, reassurance when doubts press in, and clarity when choices feel confusing. **The gift of knowledge builds confidence and clarity, especially when we need it most.** It anchors us in truth and points us back, again and again, to the One who is the source of all wisdom.

Invitation:

As you study the scriptures today, ask the Holy Ghost to give you insight. Expect to receive personal knowledge.

Journaling Prompt:

When have you received knowledge or understanding from the Spirit that surprised you?

Affirmation:

The Holy Ghost gives me spiritual knowledge. I trust that He will help me understand what I need to know.

Day 10

"And again, verily I say unto you, to some is given, by the Spirit of God, the word of wisdom."
                                    Doctrine and Covenants 46:17

When I was growing up, I thought the gift of the word of wisdom mentioned in the above scripture meant being able to follow the Word of Wisdom. It wasn't until I got older and studied the footnotes that I realized this gift was something entirely different. It's about being able to teach, to discern, and to offer knowledge with spiritual clarity. It is wisdom given by the Spirit, not just good judgment, but divine perspective.

Wisdom is more than intelligence. It's knowing *how* to apply truth. It's the Spirit helping us navigate the gray areas of life with grace, compassion, and clarity. And sometimes, it comes in the most unexpected ways.

I once watched a mother quietly settle a conflict between her children. She didn't just correct them, she taught them, guided them, and helped them understand one another. It was more than good parenting. It was wisdom in action. I realized I had just witnessed a spiritual gift unfold in a church pew in the middle of the Sunday sacrament meeting.

The gift of wisdom often reveals itself in conversation—in a perfectly timed question, a soft reply, a new perspective that changes everything. If you've ever said something and thought, *Where did that come from?*, it might've been the Spirit whispering wisdom through you. **It's not always about speaking more; often it's about listening deeply and then offering the right truth at the right time.**

This gift brings peace and insight to homes, wards, and hearts. It's how we help each other walk the covenant path without tripping over pride or impatience. It's one of the quiet glories of discipleship, rarely noticed, but deeply powerful. And when used with humility, it can soften hearts, prevent conflict, and open doors to revelation that intellect alone could never reach.

Invitation:

Ask the Lord to help you recognize wisdom—whether it's flowing through you or being offered to you through someone else.

Journaling Prompt:

When have you seen the gift of wisdom at work in a conversation, decision, or relationship?

Affirmation:

God gives me wisdom through the Spirit. I am learning to notice and trust that gentle guidance.

Day 11

"And again, to some it is given to have faith to be healed;"

Doctrine and Covenants 46:19

HEALING ISN'T ALWAYS IMMEDIATE. It's not always visible. But when it comes, it is sacred. And sometimes, the most profound healing happens quietly, inside a heart that has chosen to trust God after being hurt. That trust is itself a miracle: the decision to keep believing, to keep walking, even when the body still aches or the situation hasn't changed.

The scriptures teach that some have the gift to be healed, and others the gift to heal. Both are miracles. But today, let's pause on the gift of *being healed*. That takes faith. Not just faith to be delivered, but faith to endure, to grow, to let God work His will. It takes humility to say, "Lord, I will receive healing however You choose to send it—whether through relief, through strength, or through peace."

A friend once shared her experience with chronic illness. Despite countless priesthood blessings and prayers, the pain lingered. But something else emerged, peace. Clarity. Strength she didn't know she had. "I realized," she said, "that being healed didn't mean the illness vanished. It meant I wasn't walking through it alone." Her body still carries the trial, but her spirit now carries the assurance of Christ's nearness. That was healing of the deepest kind.

Sometimes, the healing we receive is emotional or spiritual. The mending of a heart. The calming of a storm inside us. The courage to forgive. The strength to move forward. In those moments, the Holy Ghost becomes both Comforter and Healer, stitching together the broken places in ways no doctor or remedy ever could.

If you've ever found peace in the middle of chaos, if you've ever been able to breathe again after heartbreak, you've witnessed this gift at work. **Healing is not just about what is taken away—it is about what God gives in return:** hope, strength, and the quiet assurance that Christ's power is enough.

Invitation:

Reflect on an area of your life where healing is still in process. Invite the Lord to show you how that healing may already be unfolding.

Journaling Prompt:

When have you felt the quiet, steady gift of healing—physically, emotionally, or spiritually?

Affirmation:

God is healing me in His time and His way. I trust His hands and His heart.

Day 12

> *"A man hath joy by the answer of his mouth: and a word spoken in due season, how good is it!"*
>
> Proverbs 15:23

THERE IS A SPIRITUAL gift that often goes unnoticed because it feels so natural. It's the ability to say the *right thing* at the *right time*. A text. A testimony. A phrase whispered across a kitchen table. It might be a line in a lesson that speaks directly to a silent question, a scripture that surfaces in your mind at just the right moment, or a quiet word of encouragement that steadies someone on the edge of giving up. And somehow, it's exactly what someone needed.

The gift of inspired speech isn't about eloquence. It's about alignment—your words lining up with the Spirit's promptings. It's God using your voice to comfort, guide, or awaken something in another soul. Sometimes it's only a sentence or two, but those words can echo for years in the heart of the person who heard them.

A friend once told me about a letter she received during a hard season. It was simple—just a few sentences—but every word felt heaven-sent. It wasn't poetic or profound. But it was precise. The right word in the right season. She kept that letter for years. Each time she reread it, she felt the Spirit whisper, "I see you. I haven't forgotten you." To her, that letter became more than encouragement, it became evidence of God's awareness.

You may have experienced this yourself. You said something and later found out it made all the difference to someone. Or you've been on the receiving end, and a single sentence brought light to your whole day, week, month, or life. That's the Spirit at work. **He knows what we cannot know and gives us words we could not have chosen on our own. That is why this gift is sacred, it carries God's voice disguised as our own.**

This gift reminds us that God knows what we need to hear, and He often delivers it through each other. When we yield to His whisperings, our ordinary words become extraordinary instruments of healing, guidance, and hope.

Invitation:

Pray today to be a vessel for the Spirit's words. Ask to speak something small but meaningful to someone who needs it.

Journaling Prompt:

When has someone said something that felt like it came straight from the Lord to you?

Affirmation:

The Spirit speaks through me. My words, guided by love, can lift and heal others.

Day 13

> *"To another is given the word of knowledge, that all may be taught to be wise and to have knowledge."*
>
> Doctrine and Covenants 46:18

SOME PEOPLE HAVE A way of making truth come alive. They can explain things clearly, ask just the right questions, and connect gospel principles to real life. That's not just a talent, it's a spiritual gift: the gift to teach by the Spirit.

Teaching isn't limited to classrooms. Parents, leaders, friends, and even children can teach with power when the Spirit is involved. It's not about credentials, it's about conversion. The Spirit can work through a Primary child sharing a simple song, a parent reading scripture at the dinner table, or a youth bearing testimony at camp. Wherever the Spirit is welcome, teaching can happen.

A friend once shared with me an experience she had in Relief Society that changed how she saw the Atonement. The teacher wasn't a polished speaker, but she was spiritually prepared. Every scripture, every story felt anointed. My friend said she left with a full heart and a deeper love for the Savior. As she told me about it, I realized that's what the gift of teaching by the Spirit does; it points us straight to Him. **It doesn't glorify the teacher; it glorifies Christ. And when He is lifted up, hearts are changed.**

If you've ever taught and felt words come that weren't your own, or if you've listened to someone and felt truth sink deep into your heart, you've seen this gift in action. It's a miracle of connection: heaven speaking through mortal lips, truth piercing past distractions, and light illuminating the soul.

It's a quiet miracle. And it builds Zion one heart at a time, gathering individuals into unity through understanding and testimony. It may seem small—a lesson, a scripture shared, a question answered—but each act of Spirit-led teaching strengthens the whole body of Christ.

Invitation:

Before your next opportunity to teach or testify—even in a conversation—ask the Spirit to guide your words and help you touch hearts.

Journaling Prompt:

When has someone taught you in a way that felt Spirit-led and unforgettable?

Affirmation:

The Spirit teaches through me. I am a vessel for truth, and my voice can lead others to Christ.

Day 14

"And to others it is given to have faith to heal."
Doctrine and Covenants 46:20

SOME PEOPLE SEEM TO carry a healing presence. They walk into a room and things feel lighter. They speak, and burdens seem to lift. Their hugs, their hands, even their silence has a calming effect. This, too, is a spiritual gift, the faith to heal. It's not always dramatic or public, but it is powerful. Healing can flow through the smallest gestures, like a kind word spoken at the right time, or the simple ministry of being present when someone feels forgotten.

Healing comes in many forms. Yes, there are priesthood blessings and miraculous recoveries. But there's also the quiet healer, the one who prays deeply, listens with love, and stays beside you in your sorrow. They may not even realize they're healing anyone, but the Lord is using them to mend what's broken. These are the people who reflect the Savior's nature most clearly, because His ministry was so often one of quiet presence, tender touch, and compassionate words.

I once saw a ward member sit beside someone who had just lost a loved one. She didn't say much. She didn't try to fix it. She just stayed, and cried with them. She reached out and held their hand, steady and warm, as if to share the weight of the sorrow. At one point, she gently wiped a tear from their cheek, then wrapped them in a silent, lingering hug. That moment did more healing than any sermon ever could. In that silence, the Spirit spoke louder than words ever could, and hearts that felt shattered began to feel the first stitches of peace.

If you've ever felt prompted to reach out to someone in pain, to offer a listening ear, to give a blessing, or even to just be there, you may be exercising this gift. The faith to heal is sacred. And needed. **Our world aches with wounds both seen and unseen, and God answers those aches through His disciples who are willing to be His healing hands.**

Invitation:

Ask in prayer to be an instrument of healing today, even in a small, quiet way.

Journaling Prompt:

When have you witnessed or experienced the healing influence of someone's faith, love, or presence?

Affirmation:

God can work healing through me. My faith, love, and presence can be part of someone's miracle.

Day 15

> *"But the Comforter, which is the Holy Ghost, whom the Father will send in my name, he shall teach you all things, and bring all things to your remembrance, whatsoever I have said unto you."*
>
> John 14:26

HAVE YOU EVER HAD the perfect scripture come to mind right when you needed it? Or remembered a spiritual prompting at just the right time? That's not just coincidence. That's a spiritual gift—the Holy Ghost bringing things to your remembrance.

This gift might seem small, but it can have an eternal impact. It's the sudden memory of a truth you'd forgotten. The verse that returns to your heart like an anchor. It's how the Lord personalizes revelation for your moment, your situation, your need. It's one of the tender mercies of the Lord, a reminder that He is not distant but deeply aware of you. **Even the smallest whisper of remembered truth can redirect an entire day, or even a lifetime.**

A man once told me about his struggle to forgive someone. He wanted to move on, but his heart wouldn't follow. Then one day, during sacrament meeting, a line from a talk he had heard months earlier resurfaced in his mind: *"Forgiveness is not approval. It's release."* That single remembered phrase softened something inside him. He knew it was the Spirit's way of moving him toward healing. That memory didn't just bring clarity, it brought freedom. He said it reminded him that God's truths stay with us, waiting quietly in the background until the moment we are ready to receive them again.

The Lord doesn't just teach truth. He reminds us of it. Over and over, with patience and grace. That gift of remembrance is a form of ongoing revelation. It helps us stay rooted, especially when life pulls us in all directions. It's as if heaven keeps a storehouse of truth on our behalf, ready to place it back in our hearts at the very moment it will matter most. That is the Spirit's gift: to bring back what we need, exactly when we need it.

Invitation:

Ask the Holy Ghost to bring to your remembrance something He's already taught you—something you need today.

Journaling Prompt:

What is one spiritual truth or moment the Holy Ghost has brought back to your mind at just the right time?

Affirmation:

The Holy Ghost helps me remember what matters most. His reminders guide, comfort, and sustain me.

Week 3

Seek, Ask, and Act

SPIRITUAL GIFTS ARE NOT just blessings to be admired from afar, they are invitations. The Lord has instructed us to "seek earnestly the best gifts," and He means it. These gifts aren't handed out randomly or reserved for a few, they are available to all who ask with real intent, faith in Christ, and a desire to build His kingdom.

Seeking is an act of discipleship. It shows the Lord that we're willing to move beyond comfort zones, to stretch spiritually, and to trust Him with both our inadequacies and our potential. When we actively seek spiritual gifts through prayer, study, and service, we open ourselves to divine tutoring. We learn not only what gifts we've been given, but also how the Lord intends for us to use them.

Just as a seed will not grow without care, spiritual gifts will not flourish without desire. Asking, knocking, and seeking signal to heaven that we are ready to be taught and trusted. And the Lord—true to His promises—responds.

This week, we'll explore the pattern of seeking, recognizing, and using these divine gifts in partnership with the Spirit.

Day 16

"But covet earnestly the best gifts: and yet shew I unto you a more excellent way."
                                              1 Corinthians 12:31

THERE'S A HOLY KIND of desire the Lord wants us to have. Paul doesn't just permit us to seek spiritual gifts, he urges us to "covet earnestly" the best ones. That's strong language. It tells us that longing for divine gifts is not selfish or presumptuous. It's faithful. It's an acknowledgment that we need heaven's help, and that we're willing to pursue it with real intent. To covet earnestly is to hunger for the things of God more than the things of the world.

When we seek spiritual gifts, we're not asking for power or prestige. We're asking to become more useful in the Lord's hands. We're asking to serve more deeply, love more fully, discern more clearly. These desires align us with heaven. **The Spirit magnifies holy desires, turning them into holy capacities.** What begins as a prayer of longing can become the very means through which God blesses His children.

Some people think that asking for gifts means they're trying to "earn" something. But the truth is different:

asking is an act of faith, not pride. When disciples sincerely desire spiritual gifts, they are saying to God, "I trust You to shape me into who You need me to be." In asking, they admit their insufficiency while at the same time showing confidence in His sufficiency. That is why asking invites the Spirit, because it's rooted in humility, not ambition.

One sister in my ward once shared how she prayed for the gift of discernment while serving in Young Women. "I wanted to see those girls the way Christ sees them," she said. "And He changed the way I listened." That's what it looks like to earnestly desire a gift and to receive it. Her prayer didn't make her perfect, but it did make her more attuned to the Spirit. That is the pattern: *we ask, the Lord responds, and slowly our hearts are remade.*

So ask boldly. Seek prayerfully. And let God show you the "more excellent way." He is eager to give, because He delights in watching His children grow into who they were always meant to be.

Invitation:

Take time in prayer today to "covet earnestly" one spiritual gift you feel inspired to seek. Let your desire be sincere and rooted in love.

Journaling Prompt:

What spiritual gift do you feel drawn to seek right now, and why do you think the Lord might be placing that desire in your heart?

Affirmation:

I can seek spiritual gifts with faith. God honors holy desires and prepares me to serve with power.

Day 17

> *"Ask, and it shall be given you; seek, and ye shall find; knock, and it shall be opened unto you:"*
>
> Matthew 7:7

SOMETIMES WE FORGET JUST how direct the Savior's invitation is: *ask, seek, knock*. He's not hinting. He's promising. And it applies beautifully to spiritual gifts.

The Lord doesn't force gifts upon us. He invites us to desire them, to hunger after them, and to ask for them. Not just once, but again and again, with faith, humility, and patience. It's a process, like drawing water from a well, you return again and again, each time filling your cup a little more. In asking repeatedly, we learn to rely not on our own wisdom but on His endless supply.

Asking is more than making a list of what we want. It's a spiritual posture. It says, "Lord, I'm ready. Teach me. Empower me. Use me." The asking itself is part of the preparation. It humbles our hearts, clears space for revelation, and shows heaven that we are willing not just to receive but also to act on what we receive.

A man once shared with me how he had fasted and prayed for a gift he felt he lacked—spiritual discernment. He wanted to see past the surface, to sense what others needed and how to help. It didn't come overnight. But slowly, he began to notice new thoughts entering his mind during conversations. A name would come to mind. A question would press on his heart. He realized his asking had opened the door for the Spirit to teach him in real time. Little by little, he discovered that discernment was less about sudden bursts of insight and more about quiet, consistent awareness, a lens through which the Spirit helped him see others more clearly.

The Lord keeps His promises. If you knock with faith, He will open. He may open a door to insight. To ability. To strength you didn't know you had. And **sometimes, the gift He gives is not exactly the one you asked for, but the one you truly need.** Either way, His answer is always perfect. You just have to ask.

Invitation:

Make a list of spiritual gifts you feel drawn to. Choose one to bring to the Lord in prayer today, asking with faith that He will begin to unfold it in your life.

Journaling Prompt:

How have you seen God respond when you've asked Him for something spiritual, not just situational?

Affirmation:

When I ask in faith, the Lord answers. He is willing to bless me with gifts that lift and strengthen His children.

Day 18

> *"If any man will do his will, he shall know of the doctrine, whether it be of God, or whether I speak of myself."*
>
> John 7:17

ONE OF THE MOST powerful ways to discover your spiritual gifts is by doing—by serving, loving, trying, showing up. Spiritual gifts are often revealed in a life in motion, not in waiting.

You might not recognize your gift until you're in the middle of using it.

A brother in my ward once told me about his experience with a new calling. He admitted he felt unsure and even a little intimidated at first. He didn't feel like he had anything unique to offer. But as he began serving—visiting, planning, praying—something surprising happened. People opened up to him in ways they hadn't before. He felt guided in what to say. More than once, he sensed unspoken needs and was able to respond in just the right way. Later, he realized: *this was a spiritual gift.* It wasn't something he had seen in himself before. It was something God revealed as he moved forward with faith.

Sometimes we wait for confirmation before we act. But often, the Lord gives confirmation *because* we acted. Like a lamp that only lights the next few steps, the Spirit often reveals our gifts as we move forward one act of service at a time.

Spiritual gifts are meant to bless others, and so it makes sense that we discover them as we engage with others. As we put our hearts into service, heaven puts power into our hands.

So don't wait for a perfect sign. Just step in. Say yes. Do good. That's where the gifts begin to shine, and that's where His power is made manifest in ordinary disciples like us.

God delights in meeting us along the way.

Invitation:

Look at your current opportunities to serve at home, at church, or in your community. Ask the Lord to help you recognize spiritual gifts that are already emerging as you act.

Journaling Prompt:

When has a spiritual gift become clear to you *after* you began using it to serve or minister?

Affirmation:

As I serve in faith, my gifts are revealed. God works through my willingness and multiplies my efforts.

Day 19

"Jesus said unto him, If thou canst believe, all things are possible to him that believeth."

Mark 9:23

BELIEF UNLOCKS BLESSINGS. BUT sometimes, it's *hard* to believe we could really receive a spiritual gift. We might think we're too ordinary. Too flawed.

But God doesn't ask for perfect faith. He asks for faith that *moves*, faith that reaches out even with trembling hands. It is not about having every question answered or every doubt resolved. It is about taking the next step, trusting that He will meet us there.

The father who brought his afflicted child to Jesus in Mark 9:24 said, *"... Lord, I believe; help thou mine unbelief."* That's the kind of faith that opens doors. Not flawless faith, but willing faith. Honest faith. The Savior honored that imperfect plea, showing us that heaven responds not to perfection, but to sincerity.

Receiving a spiritual gift often starts with removing the internal blockages—doubt, fear, comparison, shame. When we believe God wants to bless us *individually*, not just collectively, we make space for revelation. We show the

Lord we're ready to receive. Faith creates the opening, and humility keeps it wide enough for heaven to pour in.

A sister once shared with me that she hesitated to ask for the gift of healing. She felt she wasn't spiritual enough, that such blessings were for "other people." But one day, during a fast for a sick family member, she prayed for it anyway. What followed wasn't a dramatic miracle, but a series of gentle promptings that led to exactly the help that was needed. "I didn't heal her," she said, "but the Spirit showed me how to bring healing." Her willingness to believe made it possible.

Faith is the soil. The gift is the fruit. Start with the seed, even if it's small. Plant it, water it with prayer, and watch how God makes it grow into something far greater than you imagined.

Invitation:

In prayer today, tell the Lord where your faith is, and where you're still unsure. Then ask Him to help your unbelief as you seek His spiritual gifts.

Journaling Prompt:

What doubts or fears might be holding you back from fully receiving the spiritual gifts God wants to give you?

Affirmation:

I believe God can bless me with spiritual gifts. He honors even my smallest step of faith.

Day 20

> *"Neglect not the gift that is in thee, which was given thee by prophecy, with the laying on of the hands of the presbytery."*
>
> 1 Timothy 4:14

SOMETIMES THE BIGGEST CHALLENGE isn't receiving a spiritual gift, it's using it.

We may feel unsure, unqualified, or even afraid. *What if I get it wrong? What if I fail?* But scripture is clear: do not neglect your gift. If the Lord gave it, He expects you to use it, and He will help you as you do. He does not place gifts in our hands only to leave us on our own. He walks beside us as we learn to use them.

Spiritual gifts are like muscles. If left unused, they weaken. But when exercised with faith, they grow stronger and more defined. Using your gift, however small or shaky it may feel at first, is an act of worship. It is how you say, *"Thank You"* to the Giver. Every act of practice, every attempt to serve with what you have been given, becomes part of your offering to God.

A young adult in my ward once shared her experience in a new calling. "I didn't think I had anything special," she said. "But I kept feeling nudges to try. So I started sharing thoughts in meetings. Reaching out to people. And something changed. I realized I actually have a gift for making people feel seen. It's grown because I use it." Her willingness was the key. She did not wait to feel confident before she acted. She acted, and confidence followed.

You don't have to wait to feel ready. You just have to be willing. The Lord doesn't ask for polished performance. He asks for faithful participation. As we step forward with even the smallest effort, He multiplies our offering, turning what feels ordinary into something extraordinary. That is the miracle of using a spiritual gift, it blesses others, and it transforms us.

Invitation:

Think of one gift the Lord may be growing in you. What's one small way you could use that gift this week?

Journaling Prompt:

What holds you back from using your spiritual gifts more fully? How might the Lord be encouraging you to act?

Affirmation:

I will not neglect the gift within me. As I act with faith, the Lord magnifies my efforts.

Day 21

> *"I can do all things through Christ which strengtheneth me."*
> Philippians 4:13

SPIRITUAL GIFTS DON'T ERASE our weaknesses. They work with them. And sometimes, the Lord gives us gifts specifically where we feel most inadequate.

That's His pattern. He calls the weak to do His work. He gives power to the humble. And when we feel too small, too flawed, or too overwhelmed, He steps in and says, **"Let Me show you what I can do through you."** The Lord does not avoid our weaknesses, He transforms them. Where we see limitation, He sees opportunity. Where we see failure, He sees the chance to magnify His strength in us.

I once heard a new missionary share how terrified he was to teach. He stumbled through his first lessons, convinced he wasn't cut out for it. But over time, something shifted. As he kept trying, the words started to flow. People responded. He realized that what he thought was a weakness was actually the soil for a spiritual gift. "I'm still not the best speaker," he said, "but I feel the Spirit when I testify, and that's enough." His humility and persistence allowed the Spirit to take what he lacked and turn it into something powerful. The Lord didn't remove his fear; He worked through it, showing that the power was never meant to rest on human skill alone.

If you've ever felt that your inadequacy disqualifies you, remember: you're in the perfect position for the Lord to work miracles. He doesn't need you to be impressive. He just needs you to be available. Paul wrote of this truth when he testified that the Lord's grace is sufficient, and that His strength is made perfect in weakness (2 Corinthians 12:9). Weakness is not a disqualification; it is an invitation. It is the very place where divine gifts often take root and flourish.

So when you feel incapable, lean into it. Offer it to God. You may find that your greatest weakness becomes the very place where His Spirit shines brightest.

Invitation:

Offer your perceived weaknesses to the Lord in prayer today. Ask Him to show you what gift He might be trying to grow in that very place.

Journaling Prompt:

When have you felt God strengthen you in an area where you felt most inadequate?

Affirmation:

Through Christ, my weakness becomes strength. He can grow spiritual gifts in the very places I doubt myself most.

Day 22

"Let God Prevail."
President Russell M. Nelson

"And he said, Thy name shall be called no more Jacob, but Israel: for as a prince hast thou power with God and with men, and hast prevailed."
Genesis 32:28

THERE'S POWER IN SURRENDER. Not the kind that gives up, but the kind that opens up. When we let God prevail, we stop clinging to our own plans, our own comfort zones, and our own preferences. We say, "Thy will be done. Work through me however You choose."

Spiritual gifts flourish when we let go of control and let God shape our discipleship. **Surrender is not weakness, it is trust.** It is the act of placing the brush back in the Master's hand and allowing Him to paint the picture of your life in richer colors than you could have imagined on your own.

Sometimes we want a specific gift, a visible one, a familiar one. But the Lord may be offering us something better, something unexpected. A gift perfectly tailored to His purposes, not just our preferences. The Giver of all good gifts knows us more deeply than we know ourselves. He understands not only what will bless others, but also what will refine us, stretch us, and draw us closer to Him.

A Relief Society president once told me she always hoped for the gift of teaching. But in her calling, she found herself instead leaning on the gift of compassion, seeing others clearly, feeling their pain, knowing when to reach out. "It wasn't the gift I thought I wanted," she said. "But it's exactly what the Lord needed me to have." Her willingness to receive what God offered rather than cling to her own expectations allowed her to bless lives in ways she never could have planned.

Letting God prevail in our gifts means we stop trying to define how we will serve and instead ask, "How would You have me serve?" That question unlocks miracles. **When we surrender our will to His, we discover that the very gifts He places within us are not only sufficient, they are sacred tools, perfectly timed and perfectly placed to build His kingdom.**

Invitation:

In your prayers today, ask the Lord if there's a spiritual gift He wants to develop in you that you haven't yet noticed or desired. Be open to His leading.

Journaling Prompt:

Is there a spiritual gift you've resisted or overlooked because it didn't match your expectations? What might happen if you let God prevail in that area?

Affirmation:

I trust God to shape my spiritual gifts. As I let Him prevail, He empowers me in ways I never imagined.

Week 4

Spiritual Gifts Build Zion

SPIRITUAL GIFTS ARE NOT only personal blessings, they are powerful tools for building the Lord's kingdom. Each gift, whether bold or quiet, contributes to the gathering of Israel, the unity of the Saints, and the strengthening of homes, wards, and communities.

These gifts were never meant to exist in isolation. They are designed to work together, each one adding strength to the whole. One person's faith lifts another's hope. One person's compassion eases another's burden. This is the Lord's pattern—diverse gifts united in purpose.

God orchestrates His work through our willingness to act and the gifts He has placed within us. As we recognize and use these divine endowments, we become builders of Zion, lifting, healing, teaching, and testifying.

This final week will help us see how spiritual gifts are not just about us as individuals, but about us as the body of Christ, working in harmony to fulfill His divine purposes.

Day 23

> *"For as the body is one, and hath many members, and all the members of that one body, being many, are one body: so also is Christ."*
>
> 1 Corinthians 12:12

IMAGINE TRYING TO PLAY a piano with just one key. No matter how skilled the pianist, the melody would fall flat. Now imagine each key doing its part, offering different notes and different tones, yet together creating music that moves the soul. That is what the body of Christ looks like. That is Zion.

Paul's metaphor reminds us that our spiritual gifts were never meant to stand alone. We are not solo acts. We are symphonic. Each of us adds a note that no one else can contribute. **Without your gift, the music of Zion is missing a sound heaven intended to be heard.**

Your gift matters, not just because it comes from God, but because someone else needs it. One sister's compassion might soften hearts so another's testimony can be received. A deacon's quiet reverence might prepare the Spirit for a talk that changes a life. A mother's gift of teaching in the home might raise a future bishop, or a future missionary. A young man's patience with a struggling friend might keep that friend on the covenant path. A child's pure faith might inspire an entire family to believe again.

None of us sees the full picture, but God does. And He is weaving it all together. Our part may feel small, but in His hands it becomes essential. **What seems like a single note to us is a vital piece of His divine symphony.**

Comparison loses its power when we understand collaboration. When we stop wondering why our gift looks different, and start seeing how it fits into the Lord's larger masterpiece, we find peace and purpose. Zion is built not by one shining gift, but by many gifts working together in harmony.

Invitation:

Look around your ward or family this week. How might your spiritual gift support or amplify someone else's?

Journaling Prompt:

What's one way you've seen diverse spiritual gifts work together to create something greater than any one person could do alone?

Affirmation:

My spiritual gift has a place in God's plan. I am part of something greater, and my contribution matters.

Day 24

> *"And I fell at his feet to worship him. And he said unto me, See thou do it not: I am thy fellowservant, and of thy brethren that have the testimony of Jesus: worship God: for the testimony of Jesus is the spirit of prophecy."*
> Revelation 19:10

WE OFTEN HEAR THE phrase "gift of prophecy" and think of prophets foretelling future events. But there's a deeper, more personal meaning too, one that applies to each of us. Revelation 19:10 teaches that the spirit of prophecy is simply the testimony of Jesus. That means when you bear sincere witness of the Savior, you are exercising a spiritual gift.

Your testimony, no matter how simple, can pierce hearts and open minds. It may not feel powerful to you, but the Spirit knows how to magnify it in the heart of the hearer. Sometimes what feels like a whisper to you arrives like a shout of truth to someone else. The Spirit takes your offering, however small, and carries it exactly where it needs to go.

I once sat in a fast and testimony meeting where a Primary child stood and said only, "I know Jesus loves me." That was it. But the Spirit rushed in like a flood. It was one of the most powerful testimonies I've ever felt, not because of its length or complexity, but because it was pure. That moment reminded me that the power of testimony is never measured by eloquence, but by sincerity. The Spirit confirms truth, and the humblest witness can move heaven and earth.

Don't underestimate what your voice can do. Whether you're teaching a class, bearing your testimony, writing in a journal, or simply speaking one-on-one, when you testify of Jesus Christ, you are working by the spirit of prophecy. You are building Zion with truth. Your testimony is a light. It might seem like a candle in your hands, but in the darkness of someone else's struggle, it can become a beacon of hope. That is the gift of prophecy at work—not foretelling the future, but declaring eternal truth in the present.

Invitation:

Take a moment today to bear your testimony of Jesus Christ—out loud, in writing, or in your heart. Let it be simple. Let it be sincere.

Journaling Prompt:

When have you felt the Spirit confirm your testimony, either as you bore it, or as you heard someone else testify of Christ?

Affirmation:

My testimony of Jesus Christ is a spiritual gift. As I share it, the Spirit speaks through me.

Day 25

> *"Wherefore, beware lest ye are deceived; and that ye may not be deceived seek ye earnestly the best gifts, always remembering for what they are given;"*
> Doctrine and Covenants 46:8

ONE OF THE GREATEST blessings of spiritual gifts is protection. The Lord gives them not only to uplift and unify, but also to guard us. In a world filled with confusion, half-truths, and shifting values, the gift of discernment becomes essential.

Discernment helps us know what is from God and what is not. It gives us spiritual clarity in moments of decision, caution in times of danger, and reassurance when something feels off. It is one of the most powerful ways the Holy Ghost watches over us. It is the Spirit whispering, "This is safe," or "Step back," even when outward appearances tell a different story. It is light cutting through the fog, enabling us to walk with confidence where otherwise we would stumble.

A friend once shared that before making a big life decision, she fasted and prayed. Everything on the surface looked good, but she could not feel peace. "It didn't make sense logically," she said, "but the Spirit whispered, 'Not this.'" She obeyed, and later discovered that what looked like a perfect opportunity would have taken her far from the path the Lord had prepared. Her story reminded me that discernment is not about fear or suspicion, but about trust. When the Spirit says no, we may not understand why in the moment, but heaven always sees what we cannot.

That is discernment in action, not fear, not suspicion, but Spirit-led insight. It is the gift that shields us from deception, directs us toward truth, and preserves us from choices that could wound our spirits. It is also the gift that helps us recognize the goodness of God in others, even when the world overlooks it.

We need this gift in our homes, our callings, and our conversations. As the world grows noisier, the still, small voice becomes even more vital. And God is willing to grant us this gift, if we will seek it earnestly. **Discernment is not given to a chosen few; it is available to all who ask in faith. In these latter days, it is not just helpful, it is essential.**

Invitation:

Pray specifically today for the gift of discernment. Ask the Lord to help you see clearly and choose wisely in whatever situation you're facing.

Journaling Prompt:

When has the Spirit helped you discern between truth and error, peace and confusion, light and darkness?

Affirmation:

Through the Spirit, I can discern truth. God helps me see clearly, even in a world of confusion.

Day 26

> *"Charity never faileth: but whether there be prophecies, they shall fail; whether there be tongues, they shall cease; whether there be knowledge, it shall vanish away."*
> 1 Corinthians 13:8

OF ALL THE SPIRITUAL gifts, charity is the greatest. It is not just love, it is the pure love of Christ. A love that sees beyond faults, reaches beyond barriers, and endures beyond offense. Charity builds Zion because it binds hearts together.

You may never stand at a pulpit or perform a miracle, but if you love with Christlike charity, you are doing something eternal. Charity turns ordinary service into holy service. A meal, a visit, a kind word, or even a silent prayer offered in love becomes a thread in the fabric of God's kingdom.

I once watched a ward member bring meals, drive people to appointments, and quietly check on someone who had lost a child. There was no fanfare, no spotlight, just love in action. That is charity. And it is a spiritual gift as real and as powerful as any other. Her quiet service reminded me of Moroni's words: *"Charity never faileth"* (Moroni 7:46).

Human strength may run out, but the pure love of Christ endures.

The scriptures teach us to pray with all the energy of heart to be filled with this gift. Why? Because charity transforms us. It makes us more like Christ. And it has the power to soften the hardest hearts, including our own. When charity fills our souls, forgiveness comes more easily, patience stretches farther, and judgment gives way to understanding. It reshapes the way we see people, teaching us to see them as He does.

When we seek charity, we are not just asking to feel more loving. We are asking to become more like Jesus. And that, more than anything else, will build Zion. **Charity is the language of heaven, and as we learn to speak it here, we prepare ourselves to dwell with Him there.**

Invitation:

Pray today for the gift of charity. Ask the Lord to help you see someone through His eyes, and then act on what you feel.

Journaling Prompt:

When have you felt charity at work, either flowing through you, or reaching you through someone else?

Affirmation:

Charity is the greatest gift. With Christ's love in my heart, I can be a true builder of Zion.

Day 27

> *"Blessed are the peacemakers: for they shall be called the children of God."*
>
> Matthew 5:9

PEACEMAKERS ARE NOT PASSIVE. They are powerful. **In a world of contention, those who bring peace are doing sacred work, and it is a spiritual gift.**

The gift of peacemaking shows up in countless ways: calming a heated conversation, helping others feel heard, choosing kindness when it would be easier to argue, or simply carrying a spirit of stillness into a storm. Peacemakers build bridges instead of barriers. They remind us that peace is not the absence of truth, but the presence of Christlike love.

A member of a ward once described serving alongside a Relief Society president who had this gift. Whenever conflict arose, she never rushed to fix it. She listened with patience. She prayed for guidance. She invited others to listen as well. Tension would melt in her presence, not because she avoided truth, but because she carried it with compassion. Her ability to hold both love and truth at the same time made space for healing. Those around her often left feeling lighter, understood, and more willing to reconcile. She quietly made the ward feel more like Zion.

We need more peacemakers in families, in wards, in classrooms, and in conversations. The world thrives on division, but the kingdom of God thrives on unity. Each act of peacemaking pushes back against the adversary's influence and creates a place where the Spirit can dwell. **Christ Himself is the Prince of Peace, and when we exercise this gift, we become more like Him.** We help fulfill His promise that the pure in heart shall see God, because peace makes room for Him to dwell.

Invitation:

Watch for one opportunity today to be a peacemaker. It might be through silence, soft words, or simply choosing not to take offense.

Journaling Prompt:

When have you witnessed the spiritual gift of peacemaking bless a relationship or situation?

Affirmation:

I am a peacemaker. With the Spirit's help, I bring calm, clarity, and Christlike love wherever I go.

Day 28

> *"And if they are not the words of Christ, judge ye—for Christ will show unto you, with power and great glory, that they are his words, at the last day; and you and I shall stand face to face before his bar; and ye shall know that I have been commanded of him to write these things, notwithstanding my weakness."*
>
> 2 Nephi 33:11

WHEN WE THINK OF gathering Israel, we often picture missionaries or prophets. But each of us has a role in that sacred work, and our spiritual gifts are the tools the Lord uses to make it happen.

The gathering is not just about sharing the gospel formally. It is about drawing others to Christ. When we use our gifts—teaching, comforting, serving, inviting, testifying—we become gatherers. Builders. Lifters. We make space for others to feel the Spirit and respond to truth. Every act of kindness, every inspired word, every Christlike deed becomes a thread in the great net the Lord is casting to bring His children home.

A sister in one of the wards I attended once described watching a teenage girl invite a friend to mutual night. She did not preach a sermon. She simply reached out. That invitation turned into friendship, which turned into interest, which eventually turned into a baptism. The young girl had no idea she was part of the gathering of Israel. She was simply acting with courage, kindness, and inclusion. The Lord magnified that simple act into something eternal.

The Lord gathers His people one heart at a time. And He does it through us, through our gifts, our willingness, and our small daily efforts. He rarely asks us to do dramatic things; more often, He asks us to show up, to open our mouths, to open our arms, and to trust that He will do the rest.

You do not have to go far to gather. Just lift where you stand. Love where you live. Shine where you are. The work of gathering Israel is not reserved for a chosen few; it belongs to every disciple of Christ. And the Lord has already placed within you the gifts you need to play your part.

Invitation:

Ask in prayer how the Lord wants you to use your spiritual gifts in the gathering of Israel. Then act on the first prompting you receive.

Journaling Prompt:

How might your unique gifts contribute to the work of gathering—right now, right where you are?

Affirmation:

The Lord can gather through me. My spiritual gifts have power and purpose in His eternal work.

Day 29

> "Now ye may suppose that this is foolishness in me; but behold I say unto you, that by small and simple things are great things brought to pass; and small means in many instances doth confound the wise."
>
> Alma 37:6

ZION IS NOT BUILT in grand gestures. It is built in daily devotion, in quiet consistency, in Saints who lift where they stand and offer their gifts, however small they may seem.

The spiritual gift you carry—your ability to comfort, to encourage, to teach, to serve—is part of something far bigger than you. Every small act of obedience and love contributes to the Lord's work. You are a living stone in His holy house, placed exactly where He needs you. When each of us brings our stone, the temple of Zion rises.

A sister in my ward once apologized for not doing "more." She said she wasn't a leader, wasn't a teacher, and didn't feel impressive. But I had the privilege of watching her week after week. She would sit with newcomers so they were never alone. She helped restless little ones in the hallway so tired parents could stay in class. She always cleaned up after activities, never waiting to be asked. Her quiet pattern of service was like a steady heartbeat in our ward, unnoticed by most but absolutely essential to the life of the body of Christ.

Her gift was what I came to call the ministry of presence. And it changed our ward. She showed me that showing up with love is itself a gift of the Spirit, one that binds people together and makes them feel seen, safe, and wanted. What she thought was small was actually building Zion in ways leadership alone could not.

Zion is built by people who show up. By people who listen, who notice, who let the Spirit guide their offering, even when it feels simple. Because in the Lord's hands, no offering is ever wasted. Every unseen act is recorded in heaven. Every quiet kindness becomes mortar in the walls of Zion.

Lift where you stand. Use what you have been given. Trust that it matters, because it does.

Invitation:

Look for one small way to use your spiritual gift today in your home, at church, or in your community. Trust that it's enough.

Journaling Prompt:

What "small and simple" use of your gift has had an unexpectedly large impact, for you or someone else?

Affirmation:

My small efforts matter. The Lord magnifies every faithful use of my spiritual gifts to help build Zion.

Closing

You have reached the end of this thirty-day journey, but truly, this is only the beginning. Spiritual gifts are not meant to be admired from a distance or studied like artifacts. They are living, moving endowments meant to shape your discipleship, strengthen your testimony, and bless not only your life, but the lives of those around you.

Over the last month, you have prayed, pondered, written, and listened. Perhaps you have felt subtle impressions, remembered tender mercies, or discovered gifts you had not recognized before. Each of these moments is evidence of heaven's nearness, a reminder that God knows you personally and has chosen you for His work.

The invitation now is to continue. Keep seeking. Keep asking. Keep recognizing the Spirit's hand in your life. Share your gifts freely and with love.

As you close this book, open your heart to the Lord's next chapter. Trust that He will expand the gifts you already have and add others as He needs them. And when you use them, you will find joy, because you will be walking with Him.

May you go forward with confidence in your divine identity, gratitude for the Savior's grace, and faith that God's gifts will always be enough.

Day 30

"And all these gifts come from God, for the benefit of the children of God."
Doctrine and Covenants 46:26

YOU'VE SPENT A MONTH looking for spiritual gifts, learning about them, asking for them, using them, and hopefully seeing them in new and personal ways. But the journey does not end here. In fact, this is just the beginning.

The Lord's gifts are ongoing. They are renewed as we grow, refined as we serve, and multiplied as we act. He doesn't give them once and walk away. He stays with us, guiding, shaping, and revealing more over time. That is the nature of grace. That is the signature of the Spirit. Every season of your life will invite new gifts to unfold, just as every new calling or challenge will draw on strengths you didn't realize you carried.

You may have discovered a gift you didn't know you had. Or you may still be searching. Either way, remember this: the Giver is with you. You are not alone in this process. You are loved, known, and divinely equipped. The Spirit does not measure your readiness by your perfection but by your willingness.

I once heard someone say, **"Your spiritual gifts are proof that heaven is invested in your story."** And it is true. They are the fingerprints of God on your daily life. Quiet. Beautiful. Holy. Even when unnoticed by the world, they are seen and magnified by heaven.

So keep seeking. Keep asking. Keep lifting. Because every time you use your gift, however small, it echoes His name. Your words, your service, your presence become part of the great gathering, part of the building of Zion. And the world desperately needs more of that.

Invitation:

Take time today to thank Heavenly Father for the spiritual gifts He's given you. Ask how He wants you to continue developing and sharing them moving forward.

Journaling Prompt:

What has the Spirit taught you during this 30-day journey? How have your spiritual gifts become clearer, deeper, or more sacred to you?

Affirmation:

Spiritual gifts are the signature of God in my life. I will honor them, share them, and keep seeking His will with a faithful heart.

Keep Studying Spiritual Gifts

TWO OF THE GREATEST chapters of scripture on spiritual gifts are *Doctrine and Covenants 46* and *1 Corinthians 12*. Both provide a foundation for understanding how gifts operate in the body of Christ and why they matter for discipleship today.

In *Doctrine and Covenants 46*, the Lord reminds His Saints that spiritual gifts are "given for the benefit of the children of God." No one is left out. Every gift has a purpose, and the Lord invites us to "seek earnestly the best gifts." This chapter reads like a personal invitation to recognize what He has already given you and to keep asking for more.

In *1 Corinthians 12*, Paul uses the powerful image of the body of Christ to show how each gift, no matter how different, is essential to the whole. Just as a body cannot function without every part, Zion cannot flourish without the diverse gifts of its members. This chapter reminds us that unity does not come from sameness, but from consecrating our differences to the Lord's greater work.

Together, these chapters are a treasure map for further study. Read them prayerfully. Mark them. Return to them often. They will deepen your understanding and open new doors of insight.

And remember—this book is not meant to be read just once and then set aside. You can return to it again and again, each time discovering more. As your life changes, your perspective shifts, and your responsibilities grow, new gifts will emerge. Some gifts will remain constant, while others will unfold in seasons. The Lord adapts His blessings to the path you are walking now.

So let these scriptures, and this devotional, become companions on your journey. Each time you revisit them, you may see gifts you did not recognize before. Each time you seek, the Lord will show you more.

About the Author

Emmaline Hoffmeister is a devoted disciple of Jesus Christ, a covenant-keeping woman of faith, and a writer who delights in finding light in everyday moments. With a deep love for scripture and a heart anchored in the gospel, she writes to inspire reflection, peace, and a personal connection with the Savior. Her devotionals remind readers that holiness is not limited to quiet hours of reverence, but discovered in daily living—whether in laundry rooms, traffic jams, or small acts of obedience and love.

Her newest devotional, *My Gift to You*, continues the journey she began with *Let Him In: Daily Devotionals to Hear Him, Follow Him, and Become Like Him* and *I Am His: 100 Affirmations of Who I Am in Christ*. Each page is prayerfully crafted to help readers strengthen their discipleship and discover joy in walking with the Lord.

Before turning to full-time writing, Emmaline earned degrees in accounting and psychology from Central Washington University and Brigham Young University–Idaho, and spent 12 years as a fraud investigator and auditor. She launched her writing career in 2009 with Regency romance, and her Christian fiction novel *Left Behind* received the Eternal Perspective Christian Literary Award from the Northwest Faith & Fiction Award Committee.

Today, Emmaline writes both devotionals and fiction, weaving together faith, story, and the belief that God's hand can be found in every chapter of our lives. She and her husband are the parents of two grown sons. A lover of structure, story, and scenic places, she draws creative inspiration from her travels and the rugged beauty of the landscapes she has traveled to or called home.

Visit www.emmalinehoffmeister.com to view her full portfolio of books.

www.ingramcontent.com/pod-product-compliance
Lightning Source LLC
Chambersburg PA
CBHW011408070526
44586CB00022B/2598